WALE

FROM ABOVE

SIMON KIRWAN

TEXT: HILARY ELLIS

MYRIAD
LONDON

THE NORTH COAST

While the coastline of north Wales is mostly rural, a number of popular seaside towns line the coast from Rhyl to Pwllheli. Scattered among them are mighty medieval castles built by Edward I to subdue the Welsh. These castles, many of which are remarkably well preserved, dominate the estuaries, rivers and villages they stand alongside. The coast was once lined with small fishing villages but in the 19th century the Victorians discovered the magnificent scenery and the long, sandy beaches. The coastal resorts that developed attracted many visitors, particularly from the industrial towns of north-west England. They arrived first by paddle steamer, then by train. Though the land is relatively low-lying it is often backed by dramatic views of Snowdonia.

DENBIGH *below*

The ruins of Edward I's 13th-century castle overlook the historic market town of Denbigh. Designed by Edward's architect, Master James of St George, the castle was built on the site of an earlier Welsh fortress. In the 11th century Denbigh was a residence of Welsh princes. Edward conquered the town and granted the territory to Henry de Lacy, the Earl of Lincoln, and work began on a castle. Its great triple-towered gatehouse can be seen at the north side of the castle walls in this photograph. The castle was originally planned on a grander scale and the curtain walls became town walls that can still be seen today.

GLAN CONWY *right*

Between Llanrwst and Llandudno, the river Conwy (Afon Conwy) winds its way through fertile and picturesque surroundings. The A470 follows the route, as does a railway on the Conwy Valley Line that travels from Blaenau Ffestiniog through to Conwy. Built in the Victorian era, the railway was designed to carry slate to the port at Deganwy. During spring tides, the river is tidal as far as Llanrwst (approximately 12 miles inland) and the land is suitable for dairy farming and sheep rearing. In the coldest period of winter, sheep are brought down from Snowdonia's mountains for the valley's less harsh conditions. The Romans occupied this area up to 400AD and the site of Canovium Roman Fort can be seen beside the river close to Tanrallt. To the west among the craggy hills, Bodnant Garden overlooks the valley near its mouth. Containing over 80 acres of gardens surrounding Bodnant Hall, this impressive location is popular with both amateur and professional gardeners for its wide range of foliage.

CONWY *far right*

The small, walled town of Conwy lies south of Llandudno, Deganwy and the Great Orme headland. Edward I's dark-stoned medieval castle dominates the estuary and is met by three parallel bridges. Robert Stephenson's tubular railway bridge is furthest from the sea and was designed with mock fortifications at each end. Two further bridges for road traffic include a suspension bridge designed by Thomas Telford and a road bridge. Conwy was once on the main route to Holyhead but today most traffic passes through an immersed tube tunnel under the estuary. The town is popular with day-trippers and the castle is its main attraction. Construction began in 1283 and was completed within four years. A key fortress in Edward's fearsome "iron ring" of castles built to subdue the Welsh, the castle relies on a simple design and a prominent location. The town walls were built at the same time and these can still be seen today. Other attractions include a fisherman's cottage, said to be the smallest house in Britain, a beautiful quay, and plenty of tea and coffee shops. Conwy was founded when Llywelyn the Great founded the Abbey of Aberconwy in the 13th century. His statue graces Conwy's main square.

GREAT ORME & LITTLE ORME

left

Llandudno nestles between the two headlands of Great Orme and Little Orme. While the Great Orme rises to over 650ft (200m), Little Orme is just 463ft (141m) high. Known in Welsh as *Rhiwledyn*, Little Orme was inhabited during the Iron Age. A small hoard of Iron Age Celtic metalwork was found in a cave on the headland. The cliffs have been mined for limestone and are today popular with rock-climbers. A wildlife reserve is situated on Little Orme and the headland is a sanctuary for seabirds.

BEAUMARIS *left*

The castle at Beaumaris was the last and largest of the castles built by Edward I to restrain the Welsh. Designed by Edward's favourite architect, Master James of St George, Beaumaris is a true concentric castle with almost geometric symmetry. It saw little action apart from during the Civil War and the building was never fully completed. The picturesque 13th-century town that grew up around the castle has a Victorian gaol and courthouse. Today it is packed with brightly coloured antique shops and lively pubs, cafés and restaurants. Until the 1950s, paddle steamers from Liverpool brought thousands of tourists to Beaumaris pier on their way down the Menai Strait to Caernarfon. Beaumaris was known as Rhosfair and Barnover, but named Beaumaris by Edward I, from the French for "beautiful marsh". The castle itself was erected on low ground so that vessels might unload directly under its walls.

BANGOR *above*

A monastic community was founded here in the sixth century and the town's name is derived from the wattle fence that surrounded the monks' enclosure – *bangori*. Bangor's cathedral dates from the 13th century and was the burial site of the Welsh prince, Owain Gwynedd. During the Middle Ages, his tomb was the starting point for pilgrimages to Bardsey Island. The city's population quadrupled in the early 19th century with the slate boom and many passengers began to arrive by railway. The Victoria pier, built in 1896, can be seen at the tip of the Menai Strait. Before the Menai Bridge was built, boats would set off to Anglesey from the pier, which has now been restored. Bangor is famous for its university: opened in 1884 with 58 students it now has 9,000 – a substantial proportion of Bangor's 13,000 residents.

MENAI BRIDGES *above*

The north Wales mainland and the Isle of Anglesey are separated by the Menai Strait, bridged first in 1826 by Thomas Telford. It was just one of the many challenges faced by Telford in improving the London to Holyhead road, essential for crossings to Ireland. His Menai Suspension Bridge (top) replaced a treacherous ferry journey from Bangor across the tidal strait. Many boats capsized or ran aground, and 54 people were swept away by a high tide in 1785 after their boat became stranded on a sandbar. Telford proposed a suspension bridge far larger than any previously built, to allow tall sailing ships to continue along the Strait. Robert Stephenson's tubular bridge followed in 1850. After a disastrous fire in 1970, the bridge was reconstructed to carry both trains and road traffic. The view above shows Stephenson's bridge, followed by Telford's, and views beyond to the Lavan Sands and the Irish Sea.

CAERNARFON CASTLE *left*

Positioned on a peninsula at the foot of the Menai Strait, Caernarfon Castle is a mighty presence standing on the site of previous Norman and Roman fortifications. One of Edward I's many military strongholds, its polygonal towers and curtain walls were inspired by the Roman city of Constantinople. The Eagle Tower, closest to the Strait, was crowned with stone eagles as a symbol of imperial power. Edward's son was born in the castle and became the first English Prince of Wales in 1301. In the 20th century, both Edward VIII and Prince Charles became Princes of Wales in controversial investiture ceremonies held in the castle.

SNOWDONIA

The name Snowdonia derives from the Gaelic *Snaudune*, meaning "Snowy Hills". Sailors travelling on ships from Ireland in the Dark Ages called the snow-covered peaks by this name. Snowdonia's main peaks were also known by the Welsh as *Yr Eryri*, meaning "the abode of the eagles". Stretching from the sea at Conwy in the north to Aberdyfi beyond Cadair Idris in the south, Snowdonia covers some 838sq miles (2170sq km). The national park, founded in 1951, was the first to be designated in Wales. Its spectacular peaks and vistas bring millions of visitors to Snowdonia each year. There are more than 90 summits over 2,000ft and 15 over 3,000ft. The highest mountain, Snowdon (*Yr Wyddfa*) at 3560ft (1085m), dominates northern Snowdonia. In southern Snowdonia the two highest peaks are Aran Fawddwy at 2970ft (905m) and Penygadair at 2929ft (893m) on Cadair Idris.

LLANBERIS PASS *below*

The Afon Nant Peris runs along the length of the rugged Llanberis Pass carrying the main A4086 road from Llanberis over Pen-y-Pass between the mountain ranges of the Glyderau and the Snowdon massif. This road was built in the early 19th century by local mining companies, and sheep straddle the narrow road that is almost blocked by large boulders and stones. Climbers flock to Pen-y-Pass, the highest starting point for hikes to the Snowdon Horseshoe.

SNOWDON *right*

Snowdon is famous as the most climbed mountain in Britain, with thousands reaching the summit each week. Most follow the least daunting route, the Llanberis Track, also known as the Tourist Path. Another ascent follows the Miner's Track, used when copper mines were sited high in the mountains. The summit can also be reached by the Snowdon Mountain Railway, a five mile (8km) scenic route from nearby Llanberis. A great triumph of Victorian engineering, the railway opened in 1896 and is the only rack and pinion railway in Britain. It passes a waterfall and disused mines, and from the final station there is a short walk to the summit. Before the railway was completed, the less active were carried to the summit by ponies. Despite the large numbers who climb Snowdon, it is not an easy ascent. The weather can change dramatically and walkers must always be prepared. The most spectacular route, clearly visible on the photograph, is along the top of the Snowdon Horseshoe, the narrow semi-circular ring of steep ridges on Snowdon's eastern side.

CADAIR IDRIS *left*

At 2929ft (893m) the summit of Cadair Idris – Penygadair – is not the highest peak in southern Snowdonia, but those who make it to the top are rewarded with wonderful views. Llyn y Gadair is seen here cradled by the peaks of Penygadair and Cyfrwy (the Saddle), and the adjoining ridge that climbers follow on the Pony Path. The ridge continues to Mynydd Moel, still over 2830ft (863m) high. The cliffs are particularly dangerous at Cyfrwy, seen in the foreground of this photograph. Llyn Gafr can be seen further down the mountain, among the heather-clad rocky slopes. Cadair Idris is situated close to Dolgellau at the southern end of Snowdonia. When the Victorians discovered the Welsh mountains, Cadair Idris became a popular outing for tourists on ponies with guides. An old lady trekked each morning to the summit hut to serve tea to those who managed the climb.

ARAN FAWDDWY *above*

Crowning the highest ridge of
southern Snowdonia, Aran Fawddwy
reaches 2976ft (905m). The summit's
stony cairn is said to have been
erected by the men of Dinas
Mawddwy when they believed Cadair
Idris to be 6ft (2m) higher. In fact,
Aran Fawddwy is 43ft (13m) higher.
Both Aran Fawddwy and Aran
Benllyn, a mile along the ridge, are
associated with Arthurian legends.
King Arthur is said to have fought
a mighty battle nearby with a
giant, Rhita Gawr, who lived on the
southern edge of Aran Fawddwy.
The giant wished to make a collar for
his robe from Arthur's beard. Arthur
fought the giant and won, flinging him
down the hillside. Aran Benllyn is one
of the many places the giant is said
to have been buried.

LLYN OGWEN *right*

Almost 990ft (300m) above sea level,
Llyn Ogwen is one of the shallowest
lakes in the area at an average of just
6ft (1.8m) deep. Yet trout thrive in
its light blue waters. Around the lake,
along a fisherman's path, are views
of Tryfan's giant buttresses.

ARENIG FAWR *above*

Arenig Fawr towers over Llyn Arenig Fawr and the barren moorland. Standing 2800ft (854m) high, the summit has spectacular views across the edge of Snowdonia and Bala Lake. A Flying Fortress plane crashed here in 1943 when the mountain was shrouded in cloud, killing the entire crew. A memorial stone can be found on the summit dedicated to their memory. George Borrow, during his journey through Wales in 1854, described the mountain as majestic. Of all the hills he saw, Arenig Fawr made the greatest impression.

TRYFAN & CWM IDWAL *below*

The giant buttresses of Tryfan ("the Trident"), including Milestone Buttress, were among the first crags to attract rock climbers. Some of the most challenging climbs and scrambles in Snowdonia are found among the peaks in this range. In the 1950s the team who led the first successful Everest expedition trained on these peaks. Nearby Cwm Idwal is arguably the most dramatic cwm in North Wales. Cradled by the three craggy peaks of Glyder Fawr, Twll Du and Y Garn, the cwm is a nature reserve with unusually rich plant life.

NORTH-WEST & WEST COAST

This beautifully scenic region stretches from the remote coves and rocky headlands of the Lleyn peninsula to the magnificent estuaries and sandy beaches of Snowdonia's western coastline. Increasingly popular with holidaymakers seeking surf and sail, the region was once home to a number of busy ports where shipbuilding and the export of coal meant Snowdonia was known around the world. The Lleyn peninsula is the Land's End of north Wales, and has been a place of pilgrimage for centuries. Thousands of pilgrims made the journey to Bardsey Island at the peninsula's tip, travelling by boat across the treacherous Bardsey Sound. The coastline is home to a number of rare birds including the chough, which nests on the peninsula. Migrating birds and wildlife flock to the mudflats of the Glaslyn and Mawddach rivers. These picturesque estuaries have inspired artists and writers over the centuries.

BARDSEY ISLAND *right*

Just off the tip of the Lleyn peninsula lies Bardsey Island, a site of pilgrimage for Christians through the ages. So many Christian pilgrims sought sanctuary and were buried on the island that it became known as the Isle of 20,000 Saints. Settlement of the island is thought to have begun in the Dark Ages, but the death of St Dyfrig on the island marked the start of the pilgrimages. Remains of the graves of pilgrims can be seen across the island. Bardsey Island, also known as Ynys Enlli, is now a seabird sanctuary and wildlife refuge. The island is dominated by a large hill, Mynydd Enlli, which reaches a height of 548ft (167m). Since the 18th century, a fishing and farming community has become established on the island and today the majority of the land is still farmed. A lighthouse can be seen clearly on the low-lying land to the island's south-west side. Built in 1821, it is the tallest square-towered lighthouse in the UK at 99ft (30m). It was automated in 1987.

PWLLHELI *left*

Hundreds of yachts are berthed in the large marina at Pwllheli, the unofficial capital and market town of the Lleyn peninsula. Pwllheli means saltwater pool and the harbour has always played an important role for the town. Pwllheli was a centre for shipbuilding and sea trade for many years and wine was imported from the continent. Today the harbour is almost landlocked due to the gradual build-up of sand and the decline of sea trading in the area. Pwllheli was reinvented as a holiday town. The railway brought tourists from industrial areas to Pwllheli's two sandy beaches and recreational spots including a seafront promenade and Butlin's holiday camp. A mile up a country road from the holiday camp, now run by Haven, is the 15th-century manor house, Penarth Fawr. Built with local stones and timber and including many original features, the house provides a unique example of how the Welsh gentry lived at the time.

CRICCIETH *above*

The castle at Criccieth stands high on a rocky outcrop on the northern shores of Cardigan Bay. Reached by a steep climb, the castle was originally built by Llywelyn the Great as a stronghold of the Welsh princes but changed hands several times and was finally ruined by fire. It has now been restored and an on-site museum explains its history. The romantic ruins have inspired many artists and there are fine views down to the Lleyn peninsula and north-east towards Snowdonia. Criccieth's two beaches, with safe swimming and bathing, attract frequent visits from porpoises. Criccieth is known as "the pearl of Wales on the shore of Snowdonia".

PORTHMADOG *below*

The mile-long embankment across the Glaslyn Estuary is known as the Cob; it was built in a spectacular location, just south of the Moelwyns and Cnicht. Before its construction, the estuary was said to be the most beautiful in the whole of Wales. Today, it is a haven for migrating birds and wildlife. Completed in 1811, the embankment reclaimed over 7,000 acres of land from the river's mudflats. Tourists can take the Ffestiniog steam railway from Porthmadog harbour along the Cob and into the mountains as far as Blaenau Ffestiniog. The railway was originally built to carry slate from the mines of Snowdonia to the harbour for export around the world.

HARLECH *right*

Built by Edward I between 1283 and 1286, the commanding castle at Harlech almost grows from the rock on which it stands. Once, the waters of Tremadog Bay lapped the foot of the castle; today extensive sand dunes fringe the wide golden sands of Harlech Beach. The attractive town sits on a ridge behind the castle, with breathtaking views from its narrow streets across the bay to the Lleyn peninsula and north towards Snowdonia. Harlech Castle is now a World Heritage Site.

PORTMEIRION *above*

Built by the architect Sir Clough Williams-Ellis between 1925 and 1975, Portmeirion is an Italianate coastal village of eclectic buildings, many salvaged from demolition sites. Surrounded by sub-tropical gardens and woodlands, this unique holiday village with its beautiful hotel has inspired guests and visitors such as Noel Coward, who wrote the play *Blythe Spirit* here in 1941. Patrick McGoohan used Portmeirion as a location for his enigmatic Sixties television series, *The Prisoner*. The wide sands of the Traeth Bach Estuary lie in front of the village, with the mountains of Meirionnydd as a backdrop.

MAWDDACH ESTUARY *below*

The magnificent beauty of the Mawddach Estuary has been the inspiration for many writers and artists. Turner painted scenes here and Wordsworth described the estuary as "sublime", and comparable to the finest in Scotland. In 1869, Darwin wrote much of *The Descent of Man* in a house beside the estuary with views of Cadair Idris. The estuary runs 13km (8 miles) inland to Dolgellau and is the scene of spectacular sunsets. The Penmaenpool Toll Bridge is the next crossing after Barmouth Bridge at the river mouth. Found five miles (8km) upstream the wooden bridge, seen below, carries light traffic across the meandering Afon Mawddach.

BARMOUTH *below*

Close to Cadair Idris, and at the foot of the Mawddach Estuary, Barmouth is best known today for its tourism. During the Middle Ages, Barmouth was a bustling port known as Aber Mawddach, often shortened to Abermaw. In the oldest part of town, attractive houses nestle on the steep streets and terraces of Dinas Oleu hill, the first property ever donated to the National Trust. Another visitor attraction is Barmouth Bridge, now crossed by trains on the Cambrian Coast Line. More than 125 years old, the bridge is the only operational wooden viaduct in Wales. A pedestrian walkway follows alongside the rails. At Fairbourne, on the far side of the viaduct, a miniature steam railway allows visitors to take locomotives on a circular route and enjoy views of the sea and estuary. The line was originally constructed for the transportation of stone for the abutments of Barmouth railway bridge. Visitors can return to Barmouth by ferry across the bay.

DOLGELLAU *below*

Thought to mean "meadow of the hazels", the small market town of Dolgellau is pleasantly situated beside the river Wnion. Beyond it lies the bulk of Cadair Idris. The town is full of narrow streets, and a seven-arched bridge over the river dates from the early 17th century. Before the town became a Victorian holiday resort to attract climbers to Cadair Idris, there was a small rural Quaker community in the area that emigrated to America in 1686 due to persecution. A university in Pennsylvania is named Bryn Mawr after the home of Rowland Ellis, the farmer who led the emigration, and a museum in Dolgellau is dedicated to the story. Every July Dolgellau hosts Sesiwyn Fawr – a festival of world music.

MID WALES

The quiet valleys of mid Wales link Snowdonia in the north with the Brecon Beacons National Park in the south. Market towns such as Llanidloes, Builth Wells and Brecon cluster scenically around the rivers Severn, Wye and Usk. Elegant Georgian architecture is a feature of many mid Wales towns, while others such as Llandrindod Wells developed later in the Victorian era as spa resorts. In the 17th and 18th centuries the region was a heartland for the Welsh textile and flannel industry, with Newtown in particular referred to as the "Leeds of Wales". Most settlements lie to the east of the Cambrian mountains and have been involved in border disputes over the centuries. Many of the mid Wales medieval castles were ruined in the Civil War; others have been converted into impressive fortified manor houses that can be visited today.

LLANGOLLEN *right*

Llangollen is a dramatic entry point to Wales; the picturesque scenery of the river Dee and the rich history of the town have drawn visitors to the town for centuries. An elegant bridge built by Bishop Trevor dates from 1345 and was widened in the 1960s to accommodate modern traffic. The Victorians loved Llangollen and enjoyed trips on the canal to the nearby Valle Crucis Abbey. Since 1947, Llangollen has hosted the annual International Eisteddfod every July, bringing the nations together to compete in folk dancing and singing. In 1955, a young Luciano Pavarotti sang as a member of an Italian male voice choir.

CHIRK *above*

The National Trust property, Chirk Castle, lies two miles west of the town. The magnificent estate is entered through wrought iron gates and includes beautiful gardens. Construction of the rectangular castle began in the late 13th century on land granted to Roger de Mortimer by Edward I. Chirk Castle has been rebuilt on several occasions but still features its dramatic drum towers at each corner. The castle is still lived in today and the rather austere exterior belies the elegant state rooms with their elaborate plasterwork and fine furniture.

ELAN VALLEY *left*

Dramatic dams and reservoirs can be found throughout the Elan Valley. Built at the end of the 19th century to supply water to the West Midlands, the reservoirs are set among the spectacular scenery of the Cambrian mountains. These hills are home to one of Britain's most rare and beautiful birds – the Red Kite.

BUILTH WELLS *below*

The spa town of Builth Wells is situated beside the river Wye in South Powys. A beautiful six-arched bridge crosses the river beside the town. In this photograph, the castle mound can be seen, a short distance from the town centre. Originally a Norman motte and bailey castle, it was later replaced by a 13th-century castle and all that remains now are the earthworks. During the late 19th century, visitors began to visit the town to "take the waters".

WELSHPOOL *below*

On the banks of the river Severn, close to the English border, lies Welshpool. Originally known as the Pool, a suffix was added in 1835 to remove any ambiguity over which side of the border the town was on. Leisurely trips can be enjoyed along the Montgomery canal, or on a 50-minute journey on the steam railway to Llanfair Caereinion. Welshpool has many half-timbered buildings and the only surviving cockpit remaining on its original site in Wales. Built in the 18th century, it remained in use until cockfighting was banned in 1849. Today Welshpool hosts the Monday cattle market – one of the largest one-day livestock markets in Europe.

POWIS CASTLE *below*

Situated close to Welshpool, Powis Castle is famous for its gardens and antiques. Originally built in the 13th century, the building has been added to over the years and reflects the tastes and styles of its various owners. It now resembles a large mansion house surrounded by gardens that include terraces, an orangery and informal woodlands that overlook the river Severn. The castle contains one of the finest collections of paintings and furniture in Wales. Clive of India's son, Edward, was a previous owner of the castle and the Clive Museum, located on the property, features treasures from his travels.

LLANDRINDOD WELLS *above*

The most famous of the mid Wales spas is Llandrindod Wells, a town of largely Victorian and Edwardian architecture. Although there is evidence of Roman occupation, it was not until the Victorian era that the healing benefits of its spa waters meant that the town developed as a major visitor attraction. At its peak some 80,000 visitors arrived each year to take the waters and cure ailments such as gout, rheumatism and dyspepsia. It is still possible to use the spas at the Pump House in Rock Park. The town, affectionately known as Llandod, grew up around Rock Park and Pump House Hotel alongside the spa waters in 1747. Today there are no pubs in the town centre, but there are bars in the town's hotels and inns.

HAY-ON-WYE *below*

The ancient town of Hay-on-Wye is famous for its secondhand bookshops. They first opened in 1961 and since then many other book, print and craft shops have sprung up around the town. Hay is also the site of an annual festival of art and literature, which attracts a wide range of authors each May. The town, situated beside the river Wye and the Black Mountains, lies at the northernmost corner of the Brecon Beacons National Park and includes the remains of a Norman castle destroyed by Owain Glyndŵr.

BRECON BEACONS *left*

The Brecon Beacons National Park is named after this distinctively-shaped sandstone mountain ridge, just south of Brecon. The last of the three Welsh national parks, it was formed in 1957. Pen y Fan, at 2907ft (886m), is the highest peak in the Brecon Beacons range and is known as the most dangerous mountain in Wales for its rapidly changing weather conditions. The range extends westward to Corn Du at 2864ft (873m) and Cribyn beyond at 2608ft (795m). Fan y Bîg lies to the east and reaches 2359ft (719m). The national park is over 500sq miles (1344sq km) in area and includes two other mountain ranges.

RAGLAN *below*

Construction of the magnificent Raglan Castle, which lies south-west of Monmouth, began in 1435 on the site of a former Norman motte and bailey castle. The stronghold is regarded as the last "true" castle to be built in Britain. Sir William ap Thomas, who fought with King Henry V at the Battle of Agincourt, designed the building. He built an unusual hexagonal keep surrounded by its own moat called "The Great Tower". Initially, the building was constructed with local yellowish sandstone, but later ap Thomas' son, William Herbert, added a significant amount of Tudor styling in Old Red sandstone. William Herbert also built formal state apartments and an impressive gatehouse. The castle survived a fierce 13-week long siege, with bombardment by heavy artillery, during the Civil War but fell into ruin soon afterwards.

TINTERN ABBEY *above*

The magnificent ruins of Tintern Abbey have inspired artists and writers for centuries, including Turner and Wordsworth whose poem *Tintern Abbey* was written in 1798 when the poet was on a tour of the Wye valley. Great soaring archways hint at the original splendour of this wealthy abbey. Nestled among the wooded slopes of the Wye valley in a designated area of outstanding natural beauty, the abbey was founded by Cistercian monks in the 12th century and largely rebuilt by Roger Bigod, the Lord of Chepstow Castle in the 13th century. The great church was added between 1269 and 1301. Now roofless and lacking internal walls (these were removed in Victorian times), the abbey is a romantic and impressive sight. King Henry VIII's Dissolution of the Monasteries in the 16th century brought an end to the monastic way of life at Tintern Abbey and the building was surrendered in 1536. Today the site is owned by Cadw, the Welsh heritage body.

ABERGAVENNY *below*

Popular in the summer months, Abergavenny is a pleasant base for pony-trekking, canal trips and walks in the Brecon Beacons. Situated in the picturesque Usk valley, this small market town is the site of a former Roman fort. A Norman castle built in the town shortly after the Norman Conquest saw a great deal of action due to the town's location close to the English border.

The Norman lord William de Braose (known as the Ogre of Abergavenny) held the lordship here during a treacherous period of murder and cruelty in the 12th century. A museum in the castle's restored keep and hunting lodge tells the story of both the castle and the local area from prehistoric times.

WEST WALES

Established in 1952, the Pembrokeshire Coast National Park is Britain's only truly coastal national park and is a major attraction in south-west Wales. Its rugged cliffs and sandy beaches provide a home for a diverse range of wildlife. Islands along the coast include the remote monastic community of Caldey Island and bird sanctuaries at Skomer and Skokholm. The harbours at Milford Haven, Fishguard and Pembroke Dock gave the region strategic importance. The Victorian statesman, Lord Palmerston, protected these with a number of mid-19th century island forts. Every year visitors flock to the region's scenic coastline with resorts such as Tenby, St Davids and Pembroke, and further west to the stately town of Aberystwyth.

ABERYSTWYTH *below*

One of the largest towns of west Wales, Aberystwyth lies south of Snowdonia on Cardigan Bay. The harbour and marina can be seen to the south side of the town. Aberystwyth is home to the National Library of Wales and one of the colleges of the University of Wales. The town's two beaches are divided by a headland on which the ruined gatehouse of Edward I's Aberystwyth Castle stands. The castle decayed rapidly due to its proximity to the Irish Sea. To protect other buildings on the shore, a wide promenade was constructed, one of the longest in Britain. Along the seafront stand brightly-painted four or five-storey Victorian buildings, many used as hotels or guesthouses, and a few homes for the town's sizeable student population. Situated on the north shore is the grand Old College Building, bought in 1872 to establish the University College of Wales. It was originally designed by John Nash to become the luxury Castle Hotel, but went bankrupt before completion. Stunning views of Cardigan Bay can be seen from the hills surrounding the town. On a clear day, it is possible to see the peak of Snowdon, 50 miles to the north.

THE DOVEY *left*

The river Dovey or Afon Dyfi flows from close by the mountain Aran Fawddwy through Machynlleth to the sea at Aberdyfi. It forms a natural boundary between north and south Wales and is a dramatic region of saltmarshes, mudflats and sandbanks. Frequent flooding occurs and some roads in the lower sections can become impassable. In the saltmarshes quicksand can also be a hazard. The estuary is home to the Dyfi National Nature Reserve, and many birds such as oystercatchers, curlews and cormorants. The reserve was founded in 1958 to protect the region from the pressures of tourism and the impact of modern farming methods. Today the river is free from pollutants and notable for its salmon and brown trout. The Dyfi valley which lies on the southern rim of Snowdonia is the natural border between north and south Wales and is famous for its natural beauty. From here there are stunning views of Cadair Idris to the north and easy access to the Aran mountains.

MACHYNLLETH *below*

Known locally as Mach, this small market town has an ancient history. Situated 10 miles inland from Cardigan Bay on the river Dyfi, the town is the site of Owain Glyndŵr's Welsh parliament of 1404. Now a museum, the building is open to the public in the summer months. Machynlleth is also known for its prominent clock tower which was built in the late 19th century and is nearly 80ft (24m) tall. The town contains medieval and Victorian architecture, and is also home to MOMA, the Welsh Museum of Modern Art. Sited close to the town, the Centre for Alternative Technology offers practical solutions to environmental problems. A small community lives on site and there is a fascinating visitor centre.

ABERDOVEY *left*

The peaceful seaside village of Aberdovey, also known as Aberdyfi, is situated on the north side of the entrance to the Dyfi estuary where the river Dovey meets the waters of Cardigan Bay. It has a picturesque setting in the midst of steep green hills in an area of sheep farms. Founded around shipbuilding, the village is today popular with holidaymakers. The resort has a large number of holiday homes and attractions include yachting, fishing and golf. The extensive sands are clean and popular with families in the summer; brightly-painted buildings along the beachfront add to the holiday atmosphere.

FISHGUARD *above*

Also known by its Welsh name,
Abergwaun (mouth of the river Gwaun),
Fishguard is located in northern
Pembrokeshire. A ferry from Goodwick
harbour, a mile south of the town, travels
to Rosslare in Ireland. Lower Fishguard has
a pleasant quay surrounded by cottages
and was used as a film location for *Moby
Dick* and *Under Milk Wood*. The town has
an old fort on Castle Point and was also
the site of an invasion by the French in
1797. The invasion was unsuccessful and
the terms of surrender following "the last
invasion of Britain" were signed at the
Royal Oak pub in Market Square.

CARDIGAN *right*

Sited on the banks of the Teifi at the end
of the estuary leading out into Cardigan
Bay, Cardigan has been a seaport since
the Middle Ages. The long, sheltered
harbour meant that the town was an ideal
base for both the export of local farm
produce and slate to Ireland and as a port
for the herring industry. Later Cardigan
became an important shipbuilding centre
and the town's prosperity grew. Gradually,
the town's fortunes as a commercial
centre dwindled as the harbour silted up
and large vessels were unable to enter the
port. Today Cardigan is a thriving tourist
centre and contains attractive Georgian
and Victorian houses. Local beaches and
headlands command panoramic views
over the bay. The town has a strong
Welsh-speaking community and its
Norman castle was the site of the first
national Eisteddfod in 1176.

ST DAVIDS HEAD *left*

Situated in one of Wales's sunniest spots, St Davids Head is surrounded by wildlife. Dolphins and porpoises can be seen in the water, gannets and the occasional peregrine falcon in the sky, and plenty of wildflowers and marine grasses on the beaches and headlands. On the main promontory amongst the bracken, scrub and heather is evidence of an Iron Age settlement. A cromlech known as Croetan Arthur stands close to the remains of round stone huts and a field system by the hill of Carn Llidi. There are spectacular views from here, taking in Ramsey Island and, beyond, the islands known as Bishops and Clerks. To reach the promontory visitors must park beside the wide expanse of Whitesands Bay, also known as Porth Mawr, and walk alongside two further beaches, Porthmeigan and Porth Lleuog, before reaching St Davids Head. Caves can be seen among the cliffs surrounding the promontory.

ST DAVIDS *above*

Nestling within the Pembrokeshire Coast National Park, the small city of St Davids is a peaceful place famous for its 12th-century cathedral. The city was a site of pilgrimage for centuries, with thousands travelling to the shrine of St David, the patron saint of Wales. Legend has it that St David, born in the 6th century during the great age of saints, founded a monastery here. The cathedral was later built on the site and there is a shrine to the saint in the cathedral. A church named after the saint's mother, St Non, also lies close by. The ruins of the medieval Bishop's Palace lie adjacent to the cathedral. St Davids lies within the Pembrokeshire Coast National Park and is the only city in the United Kingdom located within a national park. The park, which was designated in 1952, includes Caldey Island (just off the coast near Tenby), the Daugleddau Estuary, St Bride's Bay coast (which includes the city of St Davids) and the Preseli Hills.

CAREW CASTLE *below*

East of Pembroke, on the flat land around the tidal reaches of the Carew river, stand the magnificent ruins of this stronghold which combined the mighty defences of a medieval fortress with the grandeur of a Tudor mansion. The castle commands a strong defensive position at a crossing point on the river. Carew Castle was built between 1280 and 1310 and developed into a manor house with both Norman and Elizabethan influences. Archaeological remains found in the vicinity of the castle, beside the stunning 23-acre mill pond, suggest that the region was inhabited some 2,000 years ago. An Iron Age fort has been unearthed as well as Roman pottery.

MILFORD DOCKS *top*

The area surrounding the natural harbour of Milford Haven developed into a major oil port during the 1960s and is still used by the leading oil companies. At 10 miles (16km) long and at some points up to two miles wide, the harbour offers superb shelter for large ships. Nelson described Milford Haven as "the finest port in Christendom". Norsemen used the harbour, and King John set sail from here to conquer Ireland. The main docks were completed in the late 19th century and the port became a leading centre for fishing. Convoys rested here during the First and Second World Wars.

SOUTH HOOK FORT *above*

After the Napoleonic Wars of the early 19th century relations deteriorated between France and Britain Lord Palmerston built, constructed and modernised over 70 forts and fortresses around the coast to protect major ports in the event of an invasion. In case Ireland fell to France, a number of forts were also built on the west coast in the 1860s. These forts have been nicknamed "Palmerston's follies" as they were never used. A number surround the naval port of Milford Haven including South Hook Fort.

ST MARGARET'S ISLAND AND CALDEY ISLAND *left*

At the western end of Caldey Island lies St Margaret's Island. A seal and bird sanctuary, the island has no public access. It is home to the largest population of cormorants in Wales (three per cent of the British population). St Margaret's is named after a chapel that once stood on the headland, which was converted into housing for quarry-workers in Victorian times. In this photograph, the two islands are viewed from Caldey Sound, with St Margaret's in the foreground and Caldey to the rear. Priory Beach, the place where ferries from Tenby dock on Caldey is seen on the left of the main island. Sandtop Bay on the western shore can be clearly seen on the right. On the far side of Caldey Island is the lighthouse which was built in 1829. The red-roofed building in the centre of Caldey Island is Caldey Abbey, designed by Penarth architect John Coates-Carter in 1910 for the Anglican Benedictines. The Benedictines were forced to move on shortly afterwards owing to financial irregularities and today Cistercian monks live on-site. Caldey is famous for the perfumes produced by the monks using the flowers, gorse and herbs of the island. There are regular boat trips from Tenby.

PEMBROKE *right*

Pembroke Castle is one of the great strongholds of Britain, used by the Normans as a base for their Irish campaign. During the late 12th century, William Marshall, a Welsh Marcher Lord, replaced the earth and timber fortress with stone fortifications, creating a mighty gatehouse tower. The surrounding walls were 19ft (almost 6m) thick and 75ft (22m) high. This strength as well as the castle's ideal location – on a high ridge between two tidal inlets of the river Cleddau – meant that the castle was a formidable defence against attacks by the Welsh. Domestic buildings were added and improved in the 13th century and in the 14th century the castle was handed to the crown. Henry Tudor – later to become Henry VII – was born here in 1547. On-site exhibitions tell the history of the castle and King Henry's story. The medieval town grew up around the castle and docks. Some sections of the 13th-century town walls still stand and visitors can still get a feeling of the old medieval town.

TENBY *above*

Quaint pastel-coloured Georgian houses surround the harbour at Tenby. At the edge of the harbour lies Castle Hill, and behind it is St Catherine's Island on which the 19th-century St Catherine's Fort stands. Little remains of the castle after which the headland is named, but the views of Carmarthen Bay from the promontory are superb. Much of the town's medieval development is still apparent, including winding lanes and 13th-century town walls. St Catherine's Fort was built in the 1860s to protect the Pembrokeshire coast from the threat of a French invasion. It saw no action and was sold off shortly afterwards.

LAUGHARNE *left and right*

The village of Laugharne lies on the banks of the Tâf estuary. The picturesque Laugharne Castle (right) was originally an earth and timber construction; by the 13th century it had been rebuilt in stone and its fortifications were further improved in the 16th century by Sir John Perrot. The castle fell into ruin after a siege during the Civil War. The Victorian garden has been restored and was the inspiration for a dramatic watercolour by Turner. Just north of the castle lies the distinctive white-painted town hall, which can be clearly seen in the photograph. Laugharne is famous as the place where the poet Dylan Thomas (1914-1953) settled for the last four years of his life. Thomas lived at the Boathouse with his wife Caitlin and his three children. Close to the edge of the estuary the Boathouse (left) can be seen on the bottom left of the photograph. The home was gifted to the poet by Margaret Taylor who wanted Thomas to remain in Wales. Whilst at Laugharne, the poet would write in a shed in the Boathouse garden; here he wrote many of his best works including *Under Milk Wood* in which the famous village of Llareggub drew much of its inspiration from Laugharne. The Boathouse is now a heritage centre; Dylan and Caitlin are buried in the churchyard of St Martin's in the village.

CARMARTHEN

above

Carmarthen is a centre
for agriculture in the
region and one of the
oldest Roman settle-
ments in Wales. A
Roman amphitheatre
remains and the Roman
walls, believed to date
from AD75-77, were
visible until the 12th
century. The famous
magician Merlin is said
to be a native of
Carmarthen and the
town has been known
as Caer-Merlin. The
County Hall can be
seen in this photograph,
built on the site of
Carmarthen Prison and
Castle. The castle was
originally constructed
by the Normans; the
ruins of some of its
outer walls including
towers and the
impressive square
gatehouse can be seen
in the photograph in
front of County Hall.

SOUTH WALES

South Wales is home to the largest cities in Wales, including the capital city, Cardiff. Newport, Swansea and Cardiff all developed rapidly during the 19th century as busy ports exporting coal and iron ore from the South Wales valleys. Canals, then rail networks, were used to transport coal to the dockyards. Coastal resorts such as Porthcawl and Mumbles offered respite from work in the factories and mines, while the scenic Gower peninsula remained largely untouched. Some magnificent castles are found in the region including Norman strongholds at Coity and Ogmore and the impressive 13th-century fortification at Caerphilly.

WORMS HEAD *below*

The nature reserve on Worms Head can be reached across the causeway at low tide. Rising tides can make this crossing dangerous and a large bell is available to those who get into difficulties. The island lies at the westernmost tip of the Gower peninsula, close to the village of Rhossili. Owned by the National Trust, Worms Head contains a bird reserve and there are a number of shipwrecks to see at low tide, including the *Helvetia* which dates from 1887. There are panoramic views from Rhossili Downs over the three-mile long beach – the longest on the Gower Peninsula.

LLANELLI *above*

The town of Llanelli is famous for its industry and its rugby. Steel, tin-plating, chemical and engineering works are just some of the heavy industries based here. Llanelli is home to the

Scarlets, one of the most renowned of the Welsh rugby teams. The team's anthem, *Sospan Fach* (meaning "little saucepan") is a Welsh folk song and a reminder of the area's industrial heritage.

WHITEFORD POINT
above

Beyond the dune and pine plantation at Whiteford Burrows, just north of Llanmadoc, lies a glorious sandy beach, two miles long at the southern edge of the Loughor Estuary. At the tip of Whiteford Point stands an old lighthouse that can be reached on foot at low tide. The journey is long and can be treacherous due to changing tides and quicksands – unexploded shells add a further hazard for the unwary hiker. Now a listed ancient monument, the lighthouse was used for bomb practice during the First World War. From here, the visitor can enjoy views across the estuary towards Llanelli.

CASWELL BAY *left*

The first major resort west of Mumbles, Caswell Bay is a beautiful area with a wide sandy beach. In certain weather conditions the beach is popular with surfers. The resort's popularity grew in Victorian times when it was regularly visited by groups of children from workhouses. Today, lifeguards patrol the area during high season and a dog ban in the summer helps to keep the beach clean and safe for bathing.

MUMBLES *right*

Mumbles Lighthouse stands on the headland at Mumbles at the western end of the wide Swansea Bay. Built in 1794, it warns ships of two massive underwater sandbanks close by. The Victorian pier has been restored and houses a café and amusement arcade. Mumbles is the gateway to the Gower coast and the seas here are popular with the sailing community. The village developed around the fishing community at Oystermouth; the name Mumbles comes from the French word *mamelles*, meaning breasts, a reference to the two islands beyond the promontory.

OYSTERMOUTH *below*

The hill on which Oystermouth Castle stands allows visitors fantastic views eastwards across Swansea Bay and west towards the glorious beaches of the Gower peninsula. The castle was founded by the Normans in the early 12th century and its main sections were built in the 13th and 14th centuries. The stronghold is now in ruins but is a popular tourist destination with an open-air theatre in the grounds during the summer months. Oystermouth was once a small fishing village but developed into a seaside resort in the Victorian era.

SWANSEA *left*

At the mouth of the river Tawe (its Welsh name is Abertawe), Swansea developed as a shipbuilding and coalmining centre and the port soon became the largest in Wales. With the decline of traditional industry, the old dock at Swansea was converted into a marina and a lively maritime quarter.

NEATH ABBEY *right*

The abbey at Neath, located to the north of the town, was originally built by the Norman Baron Richard de Granville on land that had been seized from the Welsh in the early 12th century. In the 16th century, the building was converted into a mansion by Sir Richard Williams and passed on to Sir John Herbert. It remained occupied throughout the 17th century and later became a copper smelting and casting workshop. Remains of a Roman town can be visited close to the ruins of the abbey.

PORTHCAWL *above*

Now famous for its clean wide beaches at Sandy Bay, Trecco Bay and Rest Bay, Porthcawl was once a busy port exporting coal and iron. The Edwardian promenade dates from this time and there are many historic buildings around the harbour. The port's growth was soon overtaken by other rapidly-growing ports such as Barry and so the focus turned to tourism. The Grand Pavilion was built in the 1930s and was once one of the most popular pantomime venues in Wales. It hosts an Elvis festival each year, known as the Elvies, attracting Elvis impersonators from around the world. Visitors come to Porthcawl for both relaxation and non-stop entertainment. There are amusement arcades, white-knuckle rides and family activities, as well as surfing, sailing, fishing and golf. The town has become famous for brave swimmers who face the bracing waters of the Bristol Channel each year on Christmas Day. The Royal Porthcawl Golf Club by Rest Bay is rated among the world's best golf courses.

PORT TALBOT *right*

A deep water harbour was opened in 1970 by the Queen and serves Port Talbot's steel industry. It is the deepest harbour in the Severn Estuary and is mainly used to import raw materials such as iron ore. Port Talbot has many factories and processing plants and has been an industrial area for centuries, with a long history of coalmining. The town is named after the Talbot family who developed the original harbour in the 19th century.

CAERPHILLY *above*

Spread over 30 acres, Caerphilly Castle is the largest castle in Wales and the second largest in Britain (after Windsor Castle). Built in the late 13th century by the Norman Lord Gilbert de Clare, it is an example of a concentric castle with impressive defence systems. As well as walls within walls, the fortress is surrounded by an impressive moat and a number of lake and island arrangements to deter and slow attackers. The castle also features a leaning tower that was a victim of attacks by Parliamentary forces in 1648; interestingly, it out-performs the famous tower in Pisa. Unlike other Welsh castles, Caerphilly was largely untouched during the Civil War. Much of the castle was restored in the 19th century by the Marquess of Bute.

TOWER COLLIERY *below*

The miners who worked the last deep mine in South Wales were made redundant when Tower Colliery, near Hirwaun, closed in 1994. But the following year the employees bought out and re-opened the colliery. Tower Colliery was named after the nearby Crawshay's Tower, a folly built in 1848. The colliery was founded as a drift mine in 1864. The Tower Colliery finally closed in January 2008, having worked out the remaining seams.

COITY CASTLE *above*

The embankments and curtain walls of the castle at Coity dwarf the small, quiet village. Though the castle is one of three Norman strongholds in the area, along with Newcastle and Ogmore, much of the standing stonework was built in the 14th century by Sir Payn de Turberville. Sir Lawrence Berkerolles ordered substantial alterations to the keep and castle. New buildings were added within the inner bailey as well as new walls, towers, a portcullis and a drawbridge. Further embellishments were added during Tudor times such as tall chimneys rising from the kitchen. The once-mighty castle managed to withstand a siege by the Welsh rebel, Owain Glyndŵr in the early 15th century when others crumbled. However, the castle fell into disrepair when it was abandoned in the 17th century and is now maintained by Cadw (the Welsh Assembly's historic environment division).

CARDIFF *above and below*

The capital city of Wales, Cardiff is situated beside the Bristol Channel, and is a vibrant and exciting metropolis with a rich history. A small town until the early 19th century, Cardiff grew rapidly during the Industrial Revolution and is today the largest city in Wales. The photograph (above) shows an impressive view of Cardiff's Millennium Stadium, which replaced Cardiff Arms Park rugby ground in 1999. It is the national stadium of Wales and features an 8,000 ton retractable roof, only the second in Europe. During the 19th century Cardiff's port – known as Tiger Bay – was one of the world's busiest, exporting coal around the world. The historic dockland has recently been regenerated and re-named Cardiff Bay (below). A new building for the National Assembly of Wales – designed by Richard Rogers – was opened in 2006 by the Queen. Cardiff's showpiece arts venue, the Wales Millennium Centre, stands nearby.

NEWPORT *above*

Although Newport has an ancient history, dating
back to the Romans, the town is best known for
its industrial heritage. The discovery of coal and
iron ore in the Monmouthshire valleys led to
Newport's sudden development from a small
village to a world-famous port. By the 1830s the
population had grown tenfold and Newport was
the largest town in Wales. The industrial wealth
from the valleys was brought to an inland dock by
canals and steam power. While Newport has seen
the decline of traditional industries in the 20th
century, it now serves new industries. The massive
Transporter Bridge across the river Usk was built
in 1906 and is believed to be one of only seven
other such bridges in the world. It was designed to
allow shipping to continue along the river
uninterrupted by the flow of traffic across the
bridge. The history of the docks is explored at the
Pillgwenlly Heritage Centre in the heart of
Newport's dockland.

SEVERN CROSSING *right*

The original Severn Bridge is today an icon
of Wales, forming the southern gateway from
England. Its opening in 1966 by the Queen was
hailed as the start of a new era of economic
expansion in south Wales. Until then, the Severn
Estuary was crossed by ferry between Aust in
south Gloucestershire and the Beachley peninsula
in Monmouthshire. The Severn Bridge (Pont
Hafren) was built, connecting the M4 to Wales.
It followed almost the exact route of the old ferry
crossing and took five years to build. High winds
and increasing traffic on the suspension bridge led
to a demand for a second crossing, which was
constructed five miles downstream in 1996.
Known as the Second Severn Crossing it carries
the motorway traffic, making the original Severn
Bridge a lesser-used route into Wales. The beauty
and grace of the original bridge is such that it was
listed in 1998.

Published in 2011 by
Myriad Books Limited
35 Bishopsthorpe Road, London
SE26 4PA

Photographs copyright
© Simon Kirwan

Text copyright
© Hilary Ellis
Hilary Ellis has asserted her right
under the Copyright, Designs and
Patents Act 1998 to be identified
as the author of this work. All
rights reserved. No part of this
publication may be reproduced,
stored on a retrieval system, or
transmitted in any form or by any
means, electronic, mechanical,
photocopying, recording or
otherwise, without the prior
permission of the copyright
owners.

ISBN 1 84746 240 5
EAN 978 1 84746 240 4

Designed by Jerry Goldie
Graphic Design

Printed in China

www.myriadbooks.com